THE PICTURE LIFE OF
MALCOLM X

FRANKLIN WATTS, INC. | NEW YORK | 1975

EVANSTON PUBLIC LIBRARY
CHILDREN'S DEPARTMENT
1703 ORRINGTON AVENUE
EVANSTON, ILLINOIS 60201

THE PICTURE LIFE OF
MALCOLM X
BY JAMES S. HASKINS

Copyright © 1975 by Franklin Watts, Inc.
Printed in the United States of America

Library of Congress Cataloging in Publication Data
Haskins, James, 1941-
    The picture life of Malcolm X.

    (Picture lives)
    SUMMARY: Brief text and photographs present the life of the controversial black Muslim leader who was assassinated in 1965.
    1. Little, Malcolm, 1925-1965—Juvenile literature. [1. Little, Malcolm, 1925-1965. 2. Negroes—Biography] I. Title.
BP223.Z8L574 301.45'19'6073024 [B] [92] 74-7441
ISBN 0-531-02771-6

THE PICTURE LIFE OF
MALCOLM X

Malcolm X was a very famous black leader in America. Many call him the first Black Power leader. He felt that black people should fight for their rights. He did not think they should wait for white people to give them these rights.

Malcolm X speaks in Adam Clayton Powell's church in Harlem.

Malcolm X knew all the other important American black leaders of his time.

He also knew many leaders in Asia and Africa. He thought black people in America and people of color in other countries should work together.

It is hard to believe that this man rose from a life of poverty and crime to become such an important leader.

Malcolm X with
Martin Luther King, Jr.

Malcolm X was born Malcolm Little in Omaha, Nebraska, on May 19, 1925. His father, the Reverend Earl Little, was a fighter for the rights of black people. Many whites thought he was a trouble maker. The family was always having to move. They were living in Lansing, Michigan, when Reverend Little was murdered. Malcolm was six.

After her husband's death, Mrs. Little tried to take care of her eight children. But they were so poor that she could not do the job alone. When Malcolm was twelve, the family was split up. The children were sent to live with different families.

Malcolm's brothers and sister in front of the Lansing house.

Malcolm liked the family he was sent to live with. But he was bored in school. One day he put a thumbtack on his teacher's chair. He was expelled from school and sent to a detention home in a nearby town.

    He did not mind the detention home. The couple who ran it took a liking to him. He was allowed to go to the school in town.

Malcolm at the
age of fourteen.

When Malcolm was fourteen, his father's grown daughter by an earlier marriage visited him in the detention home. Ella Little lived in Boston. Malcolm told Ella he wanted to go to Boston. Ella asked the State of Michigan to let her take care of Malcolm.

Malcolm and his sister, Ella Little.

Ella tried to make Malcolm settle down. But Malcolm would not listen. He learned to drink and gamble. He got a job as a shoeshine boy in a dance hall. On the side he sold marijuana cigarettes and illegal liquor.

Malcolm in his new "zoot" suit in Boston.

When he was sixteen, Malcolm went to New York. He wanted to see Harlem. He began to steal. He was caught and sent to jail. He was twenty years old.

In jail Malcolm felt that his life was over. He had no hope. He acted mean. He hated the world and himself.

A street in Harlem.

Malcolm's brothers began to write to him in jail. They told him about a new religion they had joined. It was called the Nation of Islam. Its followers were sometimes called "Black Muslims." They practiced the Muslim religion.

The leader of the Nation of Islam was Elijah Muhammad. He preached that God's name was Allah and that Allah had come to him with a message. Black people were lost people. They were lost because the "devil" had made them slaves. The devil was the white man. Through the Nation of Islam black people would be found again.

Malcolm read his brothers' letters about Elijah Muhammad and the Nation of Islam, and believed.

Malcolm's brothers, Philbert, Wesley, Wilfred, and Reginald.

Malcolm began to write to Elijah Muhammad. When he got out of prison, Malcolm decided to join the Nation of Islam and work for Mr. Muhammad. He gave up his last name. Mr. Muhammad said black people's last names were slave names, given to them by white slave owners. Instead of Malcolm Little, he became Malcolm X.

Elijah Muhammad, leader of the Nation of Islam.

Malcolm X spent most of his time learning more about the Nation of Islam. He went to meetings where Elijah Muhammad spoke and read his books and pamphlets. He saw black people who had been convicts and drug addicts leading clean, good lives. Everywhere he saw hope. He liked what he saw. But he worried that there were not more Muslims.

Muslim outdoor rally.

Malcolm X asked Elijah Muhammad if he could try to get more people to join the Nation of Islam. Malcolm traveled from city to city, preaching. He told how he had been in jail. He told how he had felt no hope. He told how Elijah Muhammad had given him hope. He gained many new members for the Nation.

When Muslim Temple Seven was opened in New York City, Malcolm X was named Minister.

Malcolm X preaching.

Malcolm X married a woman who belonged to Temple Seven. Her name was Sister Betty X. They gave their first three daughters Muslim names—Attilah, Qubilah, and Ilyasah.

Malcolm X's wife with their daughters, Attilah and Qubilah.

Elijah Muhammad became sick. More and more, Malcolm X found himself speaking for the Nation of Islam. Some members in the Nation were jealous of him. They told Elijah Muhammad that Malcolm X was trying to take over. Malcolm X was "silenced." He was no longer allowed to speak for the Nation.

Malcolm X
talking to his people.

Malcolm X felt the decision was not fair. His belief in Elijah Muhammad and the Nation was shaken. He decided to go to the city of Mecca in Africa. Mecca is the center of World Muslim faith. When a Muslim goes to Mecca, it is called a "pilgrimage."

Malcolm X was surprised when he got to Mecca. There he found black people, brown people, and white people, too. All were Muslims. All were brothers. Elijah Muhammad had been wrong. All white men were not devils.

"Why can't we all be brothers in America, too?" Malcolm X asked.

Malcolm X on pilgrimage with Muslim religious leaders in Cairo.

Malcolm X came back to America with a new name, El-Hajj Malik El-Shabazz. He had learned many things in Mecca. He could no longer believe in Elijah Muhammad's Muslim religion. He left the Nation.

He still wanted to work for black people. But he was not sure how. He needed time to think.

Malcolm X talked with moderate black leaders. He knew now that they were not always wrong to work with whites for black equality. He talked with white leaders about ways they could work together.

Malcolm X with Muhammad Ali, heavyweight boxing champion.

Malcolm X decided to form his own group for black people. He called it the Organization of Afro-American Unity. Whites asked how they could help. Malcolm X told them they should work with their own people. But this time they would be treated as partners in the fight for equality.

Malcolm X speaking with Dick Gregory at Long Island University.

Some Muslims were angry at Malcolm X for leaving the Nation of Islam. Some whites did not like the change that had come over him. They knew he was a born leader. They felt more people would follow him now that he was not so anti-white. Malcolm X knew he had enemies. But he kept spreading his message.

    Malcolm X's home was firebombed. His wife and their children escaped without being hurt. He knew now that his life was in great danger.

The firebombing of Malcolm X's home.

Even though there were threats on his life, Malcolm X would not stop. He felt he could help black people. He had a dream that one day blacks and whites in America could live together as brothers, just as they did in the Muslim religion.

    But Malcolm X did not get to finish his work. One day he was killed by men who did not believe in his dream.

    But those who killed Malcolm X did not kill his memory. Many black and white people keep his memory alive. They share his dream that one day blacks and whites in America can live together as brothers.

Malcolm X's funeral with his wife, Betty Shabazz, between the two policemen.

MALCOLM X

1925: Born Malcolm Little in Omaha, Nebraska, May 19. Son of Rev. and Mrs. Earl Little; brothers: Wilfred, Philbert, Reginald, Wesley, Robert; sisters: Hilda, Yvonne.

1931: Rev. Little killed.

1938: Malcolm sent to detention home.

1941: Malcolm goes to Boston with half-sister, Ella Little.

1942: Malcolm moves to Harlem.

1946: Jailed; learns about Elijah Muhammad and the Nation of Islam.

1952: Paroled; joins the Nation of Islam and becomes Malcolm "X".

1955: Minister of Muslim Temple Seven in New York City.

1958: Married Sister Betty X. Daughters: Attilah, Qubilah, and Ilyasah (Twin daughters born after his assassination.).

1963: Malcolm X is "silenced" by Elijah Muhammad.

1964: Makes two pilgrimages to Mecca and receives the name El-Hajj Malik El-Shabazz. Announces the formation of the Organization of Afro-American Unity.

1965: Assassinated in the Audubon Ballroom in New York City, February 21.

ABOUT THE AUTHOR

James S. Haskins has taught in elementary and junior high schools, The New School for Social Research, The State University College of New York at New Paltz, Staten Island Community College, and Manhattanville College. He is an educational consultant and the author of numerous books, including *Diary of a Harlem Schoolteacher, Resistance: Profiles in Nonviolence, Revolutionaries: Agents of Change, Profiles in Black Power,* and *A Piece of the Power: Four Black Mayors.*

Photographs courtesy of:
Robert L. Haggins: pages 4, 9, 26, 30, 33, 37, 38;
United Press International: pages 10, 21, 29, 34, 41, 42

Sole
Soal